YORK NOTES

Daz 4 Zoe

Robert Swindells

Notes by Jay Shipley

 Longman   York Press

YORK PRESS
322 Old Brompton Road, London SW5 9JH

ADDISON WESLEY LONGMAN LIMITED
Edinburgh Gate, Harlow,
Essex CM20 2JE, United Kingdom
Associated companies, branches and representatives throughout the world

First published 1998

ISBN 0–582–36825–1

Designed by Vicki Pacey, Trojan Horse, London
Illustrated by Stephen Player, Artist Partners
Map by Martin Ursell
Phototypeset by Gem Graphics, Trenance, Mawgan Porth, Cornwall
Colour reproduction and film output by Spectrum Colour
Produced by Addison Wesley Longman China Limited, Hong Kong

CONTENTS

PREFACE

York Notes are designed to give you a broader perspective on works of literature studied at GCSE and equivalent levels. We have carried out extensive research into the needs of the modern literature student prior to publishing this new edition. Our research showed that no existing series fully met students' requirements. Rather than present a single authoritative approach, we have provided alternative viewpoints, empowering students to reach their own interpretations of the text. York Notes provide a close examination of the work and include biographical and historical background, summaries, glossaries, analyses of characters, themes, structure and language, cultural connections and literary terms.

If you look at the Contents page you will see the structure for the series. However, there's no need to read from the beginning to the end as you would with a novel, play, poem or short story. Use the Notes in the way that suits you. Our aim is to help you with your understanding of the work, not to dictate how you should learn.

York Notes are written by English teachers and examiners, with an expert knowledge of the subject. They show you how to succeed in coursework and examination assignments, guiding you through the text and offering practical advice. Questions and comments will extend, test and reinforce your knowledge. Attractive colour design and illustrations improve clarity and understanding, making these Notes easy to use and handy for quick reference.

York Notes are ideal for:
- Essay writing
- Exam preparation
- Class discussion

The author of these Notes is Jay Shipley, who teaches English at Carisbrooke High School on the Isle of Wight. She is a GCSE Moderator and Examiner for a major examining board.

The text used in these Notes is the 1995 Puffin Teenage Fiction edition.

Health Warning: **This study guide will enhance your understanding, but should not replace the reading of the original text and/or study in class.**

PART ONE

INTRODUCTION

HOW TO STUDY A NOVEL

You have bought this book because you wanted to study a novel on your own. This may supplement classwork.

* You will need to read the novel several times. Start by reading it quickly for pleasure, then read it slowly and carefully. Further readings will generate new ideas and help you to memorise the details of the story.
* Make careful notes on themes, plot and characters of the novel. The plot will change some of the characters. Who changes?
* The novel may not present events chronologically. Does the novel you are reading begin at the beginning of the story or does it contain flashbacks and a muddled time sequence? Can you think why?
* How is the story told? Is it narrated by one of the characters or by an all-seeing ('omniscient') narrator?
* Does the same person tell the story all the way through? Or do we see the events through the minds and feelings of a number of different people?
* Which characters does the narrator like? Which characters do you like or dislike? Do your sympathies change during the course of the book? Why? When?
* Any piece of writing (including your notes and essays) is the result of thousands of choices. No book had to be written in just one way: the author could have chosen other words, other phrases, other characters, other events. How could the author of your novel have written the story differently? If events were recounted by a minor character how would this change the novel?

Studying on your own requires self-discipline and a carefully thought-out work plan in order to be effective. Good luck.

Born in Bradford in 1939, Robert Swindells left school at the age of fifteen to work as a copyholder on a local newspaper. At seventeen, he joined the Royal Air Force (RAF) spending two of his three years of service in Germany. Perhaps some ideas in *The Go-Ahead Gang* (Puffin, 1994) were drawn from his experiences in the RAF. The gang explores a mysterious dark tunnel, have the fastest sledge ride ever, and describe the time Bob and Don played on an RAF firing range. Between 1960 and 1969, Robert Swindells worked in a variety of jobs – clerk, engineer, printer and shop assistant – before training as a teacher. He is now a full-time writer and lives with his wife on the Yorkshire Moors.

Robert Swindells has written many popular and successful books for children, the first in 1973 called *When Darkness Comes*. His work, aimed at teenagers, is usually set around 'coming of age' situations, for example those we find in *Daz 4 Zoe*, and reflects the belief that people are responsible for one another. Often there is one sympathetic adult character who recognises the teenagers as people capable of making difficult decisions: consider the actions of Grandma in *Daz 4 Zoe* and Alice Hazelborne in *A Serpent's Tooth*.

His characters are required to make adult decisions or take a moral stand when the adult characters act in less moral or less supportive roles. Ivan from *The Ice Palace* (Puffin, 1992) lives in a land where the winter is dark and fearful. Starjik, King of Winter, steals Ivan's little brother and Ivan braves the bitter cold to find him. In *Brother in the Land* (Puffin, 1984) teenage Danny describes how harsh survival becomes after the bomb when the world as he once knew it is gone forever. Nuclear issues feature as the problem in *A Serpent's Tooth* (Penguin, 1989) when a nuclear waste disposal site is proposed for a quiet village.

In *Last Bus* (Puffin, 1996), Chris's new friend Andy
suggests a different way of spending Saturday – taking
as many bus rides as they can on a Day Rover. Chris
likes the bus ride idea, but not Andy's other suggestion:
shoplifting. When the last bus arrives it's a number
666. As the journey begins, Chris realises that they are
on their way to a sinister destination, and has to plead
for a second chance. *You Can't Say I'm Crazy* (Puffin,
1992) and *Inside the Worm* (Yearling, 1993), which have
a supernatural theme, are two original and highly
enjoyable stories woven around the idea that responsible
people should not seek to harm anyone.

Robert Swindells won The Other Award and The
Children's Book Award in 1984 for his novel *Brother in
the Land*. *A Serpent's Tooth* was nominated for the 1990
Carnegie Medal. *Room 13* won another Children's
Book Award for Swindells, also in 1990. *Stone Cold*, a
powerful novel about homeless kids disappearing from
the streets of London, was televised in 1997 as a BBC
Scene presentation. It is not surprising that Stone Cold,
(Puffin, 1995) also won a Carnegie Medal in 1994. As
well as writing, Robert Swindells enjoys travelling,
reading and keeping fit. His latest published work is
Smash!, published in 1997 by Hamish Hamilton
Fiction.

For more information about these and other books
Robert Swindells has written, you might like to visit the
World Wide Web site at http://www.puffin.co.uk/.

CONTEXT & SETTING

SETTING   Robert Swindells's story is set in Britain in an imagined
future of the mid twenty-first century. It is not a
science-fiction world of advanced technology, aliens
and spaceships but it is a community divided by a

corrupt, totalitarian system of government (see Theme on Totalitarianism). Power is maintained by a ruthless security force which encourages the deliberate abuse of economic and educational policies. Although it is not set in our own time, there have been twentieth-century governments and societies which have instigated practices similar to those outlined in *Daz 4 Zoe*. It is possible to believe such a regime might come to power in the future unless, as Robert Swindells says, 'we're together.'

HISTORICAL AND SOCIAL CONTEXT

Other governments

Chile life after the 1973 coup: September 1973 saw a military junta take over the country of Chile, in South America. Resistance to army rule was met with brutal reprisals, and people who supported the Popular Unity Party rather than the military junta were victimised. The junta used fear to enhance its power, allowing no criticism of its actions. With no representation and no trade unions to speak out against the poverty, physical abuse and poor conditions of work and pay, many ordinary citizens feared to speak out alone. Over 10,000 Chileans were killed, over 150,000 were imprisoned, and almost half a million left the country. Many dissidents were never heard of again – they were called the 'Disappeared'. Economic reforms favoured those in power but were crippling for the majority of Chileans, who experienced rising unemployment and costs but falling standards of education and health care. Worst of all was the censorship of free speech which was effective in hiding the plight of the masses.

South Africa – apartheid: The apartheid system of government is most closely associated with South Africa between 1948 and 1994. The basis of an apartheid system of government is racial discrimination. Segregation according to race has a long history in South Africa, dating back to 1652 when the first Dutch Afrikaner traders and settlers arrived. Farmers, and the slaves they brought with them, displaced the native peoples, the land and mineral wealth passing to the white minority. Features of South African apartheid included:

- Being classified at birth according to colour of skin and ancestry. The racial classification controlled each individual's entitlement to work, health care, education, political rights and living accommodation.
- Laws passed to give status to a white minority. The Native Land Act 1913 gave 92.7% of the land to one and a half million whites and 7.3% of the land to the five and a half million African peoples. In 1961 came segregated 'homelands' which split the black peoples into states too small and weak to challenge white rule. Settlements like Soweto became overcrowded and insanitary and the black peoples became city dwellers living on poor wages and the refuse of the rich.
- So-called 'pass laws', which meant black Africans had to carry identification showing they had permission to be where they were.
- No voting rights or representatives in parliament for black Africans after 1950, until legislation supporting apartheid came to an end in 1994.
- A demand for the right to be heard which generated resistance organisations such as the African National Congress (ANC) and the Pan-Africanist Congress (PAC).

If either repressive system of government were a model for the society depicted in *Daz 4 Zoe*, a number of parallels could be drawn, including the hope of change for the future. Public opinion internationally supported the ANC when it came to power in Africa; women united in grief in Chile embarrassed the army with peaceful demonstrations. Working together gained the support of the international community to restore human dignity to people who suffered under repressive regimes.

PART TWO

SUMMARIES

GENERAL SUMMARY

The novel is set in mid-twenty-first-century Britain and describes events from several months in the lives of Daz and Zoe. Their story, tracked in **flashback** (see Literary Terms), deals with how the teenagers meet and how their love flourishes despite the bigotry (see Theme on Prejudice and Intolerance) that separates the rich Subbies and the poor Chippies of the cities.

Pages 3–9: Introductions

Daz is a Chippy living with his mother amid the squalor of inner-city Rawhampton. His elder brother, Del, belonged to an illegal organisation called Dred and was killed by the security forces. Daz plans to join Dred – a terrorist organisation which kills Subbies – to avenge his brother's death.

Zoe is a Subby living with her parents, Gerald and Amanda Askew, in the outer suburbs. Grandma lives in her own apartment near the Askews' Silverdale home. They are materially well off. Zoe's best friend is Tabby Wentworth, whose father is a wealthy property developer. Teenage Subbies often visit Chippy clubs in the dangerous inner-city areas in search of excitement, a pastime known as 'Chippying'.

The zone between city and suburbs is fenced off and patrolled by the security forces to keep the communities carefully segregated. Chippies survive as best they can under a system of Subby oppression.

Pages 10–55: First meeting and after

Tabby invites Zoe to go Chippying. Although scared, Zoe agrees to go because she fears losing Tabby's friendship. Ned collects Larry, Zoe and Tabby and leaves the Westgate checkpoint heading for Rawhampton's Blue Moon club. The city looks derelict.

Daz and Zoe meet at the club and are instantly attracted to one another. Mick is to introduce Daz to Dred's leader, Cal. If the meeting goes well, Daz will join Dred. The club's atmosphere is tense; the Subbies are tolerated because they spend money. Larry's drunken behaviour causes a brawl and Daz, against his instincts, finds himself rescuing the Subbies in order to save Zoe. Mick is unimpressed with this change of loyalty.

Zoe dreams of Daz for months. Unable to forget him, she is soon in trouble at home and finds herself arguing against her parents' prejudices, defending Chippies as 'nice people'. Her new idealism leads to trouble at school: Zoe feels that Miss Moncrieff's Modern History class perpetuates propaganda and lies, so she defiantly adds 'brainwashing' to lines given as punishment for inattention. Daz is similarly confused by his feelings. His action at the club prevents him joining Dred, yet he cannot stop thinking about Zoe and forms a plan to see her again.

Pages 56–76:
The reunion
... the power
of love

Daz knows of a tunnel used by Dred to secretly enter Silverdale. His idea is to travel through the tunnel late in the day then put on a workman's uniform. Since he does not know her name or where Zoe lives, his plan is to wait by the school gates until she appears and he can tell her his feelings. Zoe's friends have ostracised her because of her sympathetic support for Chippies. Hurrying home, to avoid her tormentors, she coincidentally arrives just as Daz reaches the Silverdale exit. They become oblivious to all danger and think only of their time together. Working out how to send messages via the trash men collecting rubbish, they part. There is a tense moment when Daz is discovered by a security patrol who open fire. It is the next day before Zoe is reassured that he has escaped alive.

*Pages
77–111:
Trouble on
both sides of
the fence*

Zoe uses the tunnel to see Daz after he is beaten up by Mick and Pete for using it without Cal's permission. The route becomes too dangerous to use again. Zoe visits the Wentworth household and discovers they are very preoccupied. On returning home, she discovers Lieutenant Pohlman of Domestic Security waiting to question her. Left alone, fearing the authorities know about Daz, she is terrified by the ordeal with Pohlman. Afterwards, Zoe learns from her father about an illegal organisation named FAIR (see Glossary on p. 30 of these Notes).

The following day, the Wentworths are exposed as members of FAIR. Tabby has left school and the family are to be expelled from Silverdale with the loss of citizen status. Another shock awaits as Zoe discovers that her own parents have sold their home and business and are moving the family to Peacehaven, away from any link to the Wentworths and FAIR. Zoe questions the social and moral values that govern the society she lives in and determines to run away and find Daz.

Whilst drinking heavily at a club, Daz overhears two Dred members planning to ambush the Wentworths, steal their belongings and leave them for dead as they depart from Silverdale. For Zoe, he decides to recover Del's gun and stop the ambush. He readily accepts that he will have to kill to save the Wentworths.

*Pages
112–165:
Together –
love triumphs
against all
odds*

Zoe escapes from Silverdale by stowing away under a trash truck. The sense of adventure soon dissipates when she arrives at the Rawhampton dump and is overwhelmed by panic. The reality of such poverty is a shock and Zoe is totally unprepared for the degree of neglect she encounters as she walks to the city. Neighbourhood children recognise her as a Subby and taunt her as an outsider. Meeting Daz and his mother does nothing to dispel her sense of fear and desolation.

Their apartment is shabby and insanitary. Having spent a cold night in the flat, Daz sets off to see Mr James, the only person Daz trusts. Mr James is a Subby teacher and a member of FAIR, and he agrees to hide Zoe at the school even though her presence there is a danger. In a letter smuggled to Zoe, we learn that Grandma was the founding member of FAIR and must become its leader again. The letter also contains a map showing a safe house in Clanton Hills where they are to go.

When Domestic Security arrives to search the school, Zoe bravely escapes by joining the surge of children rushing from the building and makes her way back to the Barraclough apartment. Daz faces more problems, as Dred suspect he killed Pete and intend to avenge the death.

Whilst Zoe is outwitting the police, Dred come for Daz. He hides in the basement and, though cornered, is safe until Zoe is captured by Dred and used as ransom. Pohlman arrives just as Cal is about to torture Daz. In the ensuing gunfight, Zoe and Daz make their escape. Miraculously, both are unscathed and arrive on Pinkney Hill, overlooking the city as dawn breaks; seen from a distance in the half-light, the city and the suburbs merge into one.

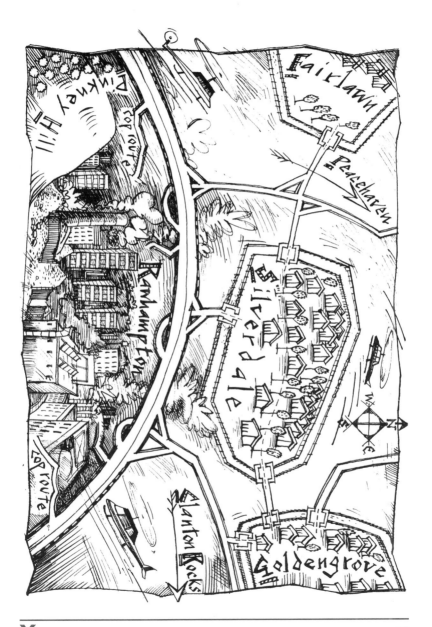

DETAILED SUMMARIES

Compare the appeal 'if we're together. All of us.' with Grandma's quotation on p. 152.
Pages 1 and 2 are given the title 'A True Story'. Written in the style of a fable, the prologue asks the reader to consider a moral dilemma: should society value material things or should society value people? What authority should decide on justice and the common good? This dilemma is echoed throughout the novel.

INTRODUCTIONS (PAGES 3–9)

The novel opens in conversational style with Daz addressing the reader. We discover something of his past life. In his society there is little work, no money, no decent housing, not even running water, and no prospect of change. He lives with his mother, who suffers from depression. Del, his elder brother, was killed by the security forces because he belonged to an illegal organisation called Dred. At fifteen, Daz is old enough to join Dred and wants revenge for his brother's

Consider Daz's motives for lying to his mother.
death. Membership of Dred is against his mother's wishes but Daz feels he has no other option. Dred at least gives an outlet for the anger and frustration felt by Chippy teenagers.

What devices does the author use to engage the reader and to highlight prejudices?
Zoe Askew is a bored fourteen-year-old whose father is an estate agent. Her best friend is the rich Tabitha Wentworth, the daughter of a very wealthy property developer. To alleviate the boredom of their comfortable, safe, organised lives, teenage Subbies often venture into the dangerous inner-city areas in search of excitement at the Chippy clubs. These journeys are known as 'Chippying'.

COMMENT The most important feature to note is that Daz and Zoe are together at the opening of the story. The author manages to create a story of human interest by balancing prejudice and alienation with love and loyalty; tempering anger with humour, and incorporating teenage rebellion against authority. Pages 3–9 give us the opportunity to experience the voice (see Literary Terms) of each character and learn a little of the lives they lead.

We get a sense of the characters who will narrate the story as they retell events from their recent past. We are also introduced to some of the terminology we need to understand if we are to make sense of what the characters say about themselves, the environments they live in, and their attitudes towards the authorities who govern their lives.

- Daz is bright but lacks education – therefore his version of events is told in simple colloquial (see Literary Terms) language in the present tense.
- Zoe, though younger, has a more sophisticated command of language and through her chapters we learn that the events are being recounted, that they have already happened.
- A passing reference is made to a Rawhampton teacher, Mr James, seen also as a figure of authority.

GLOSSARY   lornorders   police officers

dulleye   euphemism (see Literary Terms) for clinical depression

kill the goose that lays the golden eggs   sacrifice long-term
advantage for short-term gain

graft   work

veezavill   slang for restricted area which requires a visa for
entry

doodys   clothes

dazzlers   floodlights

TEST YOURSELF (Pages 3–9)

A Identify the speaker.

1 'dont you never go of wiv no Dred'

4 'We do wot we can rite'

2 'but I never crost my hart'

3 'And they hate us'

Identify the person 'to whom' this comment refers.

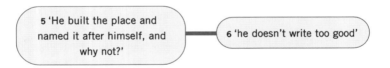

5 'He built the place and named it after himself, and why not?'

6 'he doesn't write too good'

Check your answers on page 69.

B Consider these issues.

a The moods established by the author.

b Zoe's 'typical' Subby attitude.

c Daz's 'typical' Chippy attitude.

d The poverty of the Chippies.

e The purpose of the references to hate and envy.

FIRST MEETING AND AFTER (PAGES 10–55)

Pages 10–19   This section creates a sense of excitement and sets the
                    scene for Daz and Zoe to meet. One Friday shortly
                    before term ends for the summer holidays, Tabby
                    invites Zoe Chippying. Most teenagers return home
                    safely from a trip to the city but there is always the risk
                    that a group might not. This potential danger adds
                    spice to the forbidden journeys. Although scared, Zoe
                    agrees to go because she fears losing Tabby's friendship
                    more than she fears the Chippies. Sixth-former Ned
                    Volsted drives the car, collects Larry Turner, Zoe and
                    Tabby, and on the pretence of visiting Zoe's cousin,
                    cruises out of the Westgate checkpoint and heads for
                    Rawhampton. The city is even more tawdry and
                    desolate than Zoe had imagined.

                    Daz is at the Blue Moon club with Mick, to meet
                    Dred's leader Cal. If the meeting goes well he will
Think of some   join Dred – a terrorist organisation consisting of
reasons why Daz   Chippies who have pledged to kill Subbies. Daz
does not try at   reflects on the inadequacy of the education system
school.   which offers the pretence of a way to escape from city
                    life. Dred seems his only real hope of achieving social
                    status.

COMMENT   We see the stark contrast between the city and
                    suburb environments. Zoe is appalled by the derelict
                    streets, vagrant children and the resentful eyes of the
                    people. The descriptive adjectives themselves are dark
                    and negative. Even the use of **black humour** (see
                    Literary Terms) emphasises how poor Chippies are.
                    Note the club's **symbolic** (see Literary Terms) name,
                    possibly taken from the phrase 'once in a blue moon',
                    suggesting a very rare occurrence. After all, the fantastic
                    chance of Daz and Zoe meeting in this way is very
                    unlikely.

GLOSSARY do a little coke take cocaine

Silverdale Selectman recipient of prestigious local award for civic service

PAL a brand of tinned dog food

twindeck equipment for playing vinyl records – two turntables side by side

lobotomiser alcoholic drink

Pages 20–28

What is it about Zoe that causes Daz to notice her?

Upon entering the Blue Moon club, Zoe is attracted to a boy across the room. The boy is Daz. Their eyes meet and the attraction is mutual. The romantic moment is interrupted as Cal arrives. Cal is a Chippy hero, a renegade fighting against Subby authority. Daz expects to meet a stereotypical, charismatic, handsome, courageous giant, so he is rather disappointed to find that Cal is a nervous, short, bespectacled man wearing a suit.

Consider how the author creates an atmosphere of anger and resentment.

The atmosphere is tense; the Subbies are unwelcome in the Blue Moon but their presence is tolerated because they spend money. Zoe samples an alcoholic drink. Again she acts against her better judgement because she feels the need to fit in. Larry makes a drunken pass at a Chippy girl and a fight breaks out.

Daz should fight against the Subbies but instead finds himself rescuing them. He is confused because he is attracted to Zoe, and risks throwing away his chance to join Dred in order to save her, and amazed that Cal has run at the first sign of trouble.

COMMENT Through these pages we enter a futuristic *Romeo and Juliet* type of romance where, across a crowded dance floor, sworn enemies fall in love at first sight (see Theme on Love). The moment of tension when the fight breaks out in the Blue Moon is understandable – Chippy life is hard enough to bear without arrogant Subby insults. The barely suppressed hatred erupts. It also creates sympathy for the characters' situations. Long-held prejudices are challenged when Daz rescues the Subbies.

GLOSSARY **Waterford Crystal** clear, colourless flint glass from the Republic of Ireland

Pages 29–55 Safely home, Zoe cannot get the memory of Daz out of her mind. She realises it would be virtually impossible for them to meet again, yet yearns to see him once more. Unable to shake off her romantic feelings, she seeks counsel from Grandma, who wisely cautions her to wait and see if Daz feels the same way. Her feelings deepen over a period of months and by October cause her problems at home: Zoe finds herself arguing against her parents' prejudices and defending Chippies *Think about what* as nice people doing the best they can. The new *causes Zoe to* perspective that led to trouble at home leads to trouble *question how* at school, in Miss Moncrieff's Modern History class. *society is divided.* Zoe feels that the Modern History class perpetuates lies and propaganda and so defiantly adds the word 'brainwashing' to lines given as punishment for inattention. Miss Moncrieff is incensed and writes to Zoe's parents. Once they are involved, the problem intensifies. Zoe's gesture of defiance is growing out of all proportion but, because she has taken a stand against the government's divisive economic and educational strategies, she feels obliged to defend her point of view. Through her anger she comes to realise that a less vocal resistance will be more effective, so offers the words of apology.

Daz is similarly confused by his feelings. His action at the club prevents him becoming a member of Dred, and he cannot stop thinking about Zoe. Daz is
Notice how clearly Daz thinks through his plan.
restless – he has been expelled from school, he is unemployed and he has nothing to occupy him except thoughts of Zoe. Remembering a secret he was once told about a tunnel to Silverdale, he forms a plan in an attempt to see Zoe again.

C OMMENT We find out more about the characters and their changing feelings. Despite the background of teenage rebellion against adult authority, there is evidence of a grudging respect for adults who care. For example, Daz frequently refers to events, conversations and lessons involving Mr James's teaching and opinions; and, needing sympathy and kindness, Zoe seeks Grandma's advice. Zoe wants to meet Daz again and challenges the unfairness of the prejudicial rules that keep them apart (see Theme on Prejudice and Intolerance). Here we experience the concern of a father for a teenage daughter. Mr Askew is a settled member of society, quite happy with the world he lives in. He is offended by her rebellion and doesn't understand what drives Zoe to question their lifestyle. This is hardly surprising
How sympathetic would Zoe's family be to her relationship with Daz?
since she has been so secretive about Daz. He sees her anger as a teenage phase and supports Miss Moncrieff; Zoe feels isolated. By the end of this section we see some hope that the two young lovers will meet again despite the difficulties which seem almost impossible to overcome.

GLOSSARY

got all her marbles has all her mental faculties

'Love Hurts' popular song released by the Everly Brothers in the
   1960s and covered by (among others) Don McLean in the
   1970s and Roy Orbison in 1989

savvy understanding

Franchise Bill proposed law about who would have the right to
   vote in state elections

gorgon a creature from Greek mythology. Her gaze would turn
   anyone who looked at her into stone

seeit identification

A *Identify the speaker.*

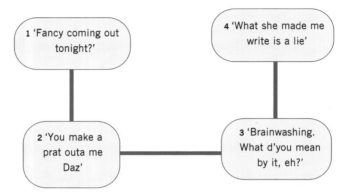

1 'Fancy coming out tonight?'

4 'What she made me write is a lie'

2 'You make a prat outa me Daz'

3 'Brainwashing. What d'you mean by it, eh?'

Identify the person 'to whom' this comment refers.

5 'Five foot frag-all wiv blond hair and neat doodies like a Subby'

6 'Her savvy's out to lunch'

Check your answers on page 69.

 B *Consider these issues.*

a Why Subbies go Chippying.

b How Cal's behaviour is affected by the reward for his arrest.

c The way in which the author develops the relationship between Daz and Zoe.

d The reasons why Zoe decides to talk through her problems with Grandma.

e How significant the conflict is between Zoe and Miss Moncrieff.

THE REUNION ... THE POWER OF LOVE (PAGES 56–76)

Daz's plan requires him to buy a workman's uniform, a blue baseball cap and blue overalls with a yellow disc, so he will look less conspicuous in Silverdale, then travel through the tunnel – probably an old sewer – late in the day. Since he does not know where Zoe lives, or even her name, he plans to wait by the school gates until she appears and he can tell her how he feels. Daz remembers learning the story of the Minotaur and the maze of Greek mythology so takes along string and a torch. By paying out the string as he goes, he can return to his starting point by following the string back out of the tunnel again.

Notice how well Daz describes the journey and his feelings.

The trip through the tunnel is very unpleasant. His imagination plays tricks on him, but his need to find Zoe drives him on. Even the gruesome discovery of a skeleton does not stop him. As he waits at the tunnel exit an amazing thing happens: Zoe arrives. Her friends have turned against her, ostracised her, because of her voiced support for Chippies. Hurrying home across the waste ground, to avoid her tormentors, she runs into Daz. They are oblivious to all danger and think only of their time together; for them the meeting is magical.

THE REUNION ... THE POWER OF LOVE

After working out how to send messages via the trash men collecting rubbish, they part. There is a tense moment when Daz is discovered by a security patrol who open fire. He escapes, but it is the next day before Zoe is reassured that he is alive and unharmed. Once home, Daz is confronted and subsequently beaten up by Mick and someone later identified as Pete because he has used the tunnel without Cal's permission. Daz has become an outcast persecuted by Dred.

COMMENT

The author uses conversational tone to effectively engage the reader. It is easy to imagine taking the journey with Daz because of the way he encourages himself with throwaway comments and because of the sensory perceptions and asides, the little voice in his head, which gives us images to share. The sense of tension mounts: the darkness of the tunnel, the smells,

How does the pace of the story change at this point?

the rats and the sounds, and the uncertainty of what he will find at the other end. The scream at finding the skeleton releases the mounting anxiety. The scene is set for the chance meeting with Zoe. Conveniently, Zoe has escaped from the name-calling by taking a different route home across the waste ground where the tunnel comes out. This not only allows her to meet Daz but gives us the opportunity to absorb some environmental detail. The innocent meeting of two people in love becomes sinister: the suburbs are securely fenced in; Daz has risked his life to be there, a fact which is emphasised by guards shooting at him and the indifferent news report perversely claiming he is suspicious, armed and dangerous – propaganda aimed at keeping the societies apart. The violence continues as this section ends with Daz in trouble with Dred. The one point of hope is the introduction of a line of communication via the trash truck crews.

Notice that there is a slight discrepancy with the days mentioned in this section – Daz states that he sets off for the tunnel on 'Fursday afternoon' (p. 56), whereas we are told by Zoe on p. 59 that it is Wednesday, which is the night of the week when she goes to youth club with Tabby.

GLOSSARY   scrip prescription
miner tour Minotaur, a creature (half man, half bull) in Greek mythology which was confined to a labyrinth
fireweed a plant which thrives on burnt land, such as rosebay willowherb
plenty of tenterhooks (on tenterhooks) suspense or agitation caused by uncertainty

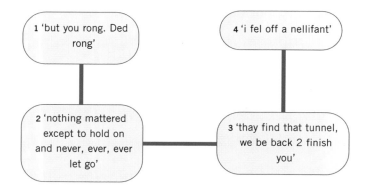

A Identify the speaker.

1 'but you rong. Ded rong'

4 'i fel off a nellifant'

2 'nothing mattered except to hold on and never, ever, ever let go'

3 'thay find that tunnel, we be back 2 finish you'

Identify the person 'to whom' this comment refers.

5 'She's down wiv the dulleye as usual'

6 'My brother. He was fifteen'

Check your answers on page 69.

B Consider these issues.

a The risks Daz is willing to take to be with Zoe.

b What you find realistic about the fears and imaginings Daz experiences in the tunnel.

c The way the author uses **black humour** (see Literary Terms) in this section.

d Zoe's reactions to the sound of auto rifle fire.

e How to link Daz's escape from the security patrol to other parts of the novel where escape from dangerous situations occurs.

TROUBLE ON BOTH SIDES OF THE FENCE (PAGES 77–111)

Pages 77–87   On the Saturday following their eventful meeting the lovers exchange messages via the trash crew boss. Zoe visits the Wentworth household to find they are preoccupied and suspicious, so chooses not to share her story about Daz. On returning home, she discovers Lieutenant Pohlman of Domestic Security waiting to question her. Her parents are hurried away and she is left alone with Pohlman. Naturally enough, she fears the authorities know about Daz. Though terrified by the ordeal, Zoe is relieved to find out that the questioning is about school and her friendship with Tabby. Zoe is surprised that Domestic Security were not as all-knowing as their image suggests. This sense of relief allows her to stand up to the interrogation.

Identify the features of language used to build pace and tension.   When Domestic Security leave, Zoe's parents demand to know what she has done to merit police investigation. In an angry outburst by her father, Zoe is told about an illegal organisation named FAIR. Rebelling against the bias of her society, Zoe is even more determined to see Daz the following day, unaware that use of the tunnel is proscribed. Daz is just as determined to meet Zoe, regardless of personal danger.

COMMENT   The author plays on our curiosity by giving us clues as to what will happen next. Zoe notices the maid Zena is missing, the nervousness of Mr Wentworth and the difference in Tabby's attitude but dismisses these facts.

At home, the meeting with Pohlman is terrifying. His vicious attitude and threatening behaviour serve to create an atmosphere of fear. We are given some indication of the power of the secret police. Pohlman is secretly investigating the Wentworths but the veiled threats about loss of citizenship are directed at the Askews. His job is to strengthen the divide between

Chippies and Subbies, but his attitude strengthens Zoe's resolve to be with Daz.

Mr Askew's reaction is to clamp down on Zoe's freedom in an effort to protect his family from further scrutiny. His concern illustrates how quickly rumour and speculation can prejudice opinion. He fears that being linked with FAIR, an illegal Subby organisation trying to improve conditions for Chippies, will damage his business.

GLOSSARY

Domestic Security (DS) the secret police

FAIR Fraternal Alliance for Integration through Reunification

Integration bringing together of persons previously segregated

Reunification restoration to a political unity

pinkos people with socialist tendencies seeking a classless state

Pages 88–101 On Sunday, Zoe escapes on the pretence of visiting Tabby. Although grounded, her parents give in to the visit because the Wentworths' phone has been disconnected. Fearing at every step that Domestic Security will stop her, Zoe's trip through the tunnel is as tense as Daz's, but her resolve is strengthened by her need to be with Daz.

How much more important has Zoe's friendship with Tabby become?

By Monday, a thoroughly upset Zoe has another shock – Tabby has left school. Truanting, Zoe risks apprehension by the police to talk to her friend, and in an effort to comfort Tabby tells her all about her relationship with Daz. She learns that the Wentworths have been exposed as members of FAIR and are being expelled from Silverdale with the loss of citizen status. This is the moment when Zoe truly rebels against the unfairness of their society.

At home she discovers that her father, fearful that his business reputation will be tarnished by association with the Wentworths, has sold the house and his business and by Friday they will be one hundred miles away in Peacehaven.

COMMENT

Notice how the two lovers, faced with separation, discuss the political climate which keeps them apart. We see the warmth of personal relationships, people treating others as equals, in contrast with the cold distance of a government which deals only in power. FAIR is an **acronym** (see Literary Terms) and an **ironic pun** (see Literary Terms). Life in this futuristic world is not only unfair but unjust. Events lead Zoe to question the wisdom of the rules that govern the society she lives in. We discover how fragile reputation is and see Mr Askew's concern now extends outside his daughter's welfare to his own business survival. He is so afraid of public opinion that he determines to leave Silverdale as quickly as possible.

GLOSSARY

den small room for pursuing a hobby
schlepped dragged slowly with great effort
wipe the slate clean cancel the record of past offences

TROUBLE ON BOTH SIDES OF THE FENCE

Pages *104–106 &* *108–109* *Where does Zoe learn of this escape route?*	Turning to Grandma for consolation, Zoe is disappointed that the old lady will not let her move in and can offer no comforting solution. Zoe does not understand why the family needs to move to Peacehaven and, rather than leave with them, rashly determines to run away and live with Daz. She escapes as a stowaway hiding under a trash truck. Naïvely, she does not fully consider the implications of her actions. She is unprepared for life outside the protection of her home, yet realises she will be totally dependent on Daz.

COMMENT   This section is a turning point in terms of the pace (see Literary Terms) of the novel. Zoe is faced with adult emotions but still reacts as a child and turns to Grandma for support. Zoe naïvely expects her problem to be solved by moving into Grandma's apartment and is bitterly upset when this option is denied her. Notice how the author offers us another clue to wider issues when Grandma almost lets slip her connection with FAIR: 'Just when we —'. Zoe is too preoccupied with her own troubles to notice. By page 109, Zoe has made a plan to run away.

Pages *102–103, 107* *& 110–111* *How does Daz justify shooting Pete?*	Trying to drown his sorrows on Sunday night, Daz overhears two Dred members – one of them Pete – planning to ambush the Wentworths, steal their belongings and leave them for dead, as they leave Silverdale on Tuesday. For Zoe's sake, he decides to stop the ambush and accepts rather matter-of-factly that he will have to kill in order to do so. He recovers Del's gun from its hiding place, and spends a cold night waiting for the ambushers. When he decides there is no point in delaying, Daz shoots Pete with little emotion, even though he has never killed before, and goes home for breakfast.

COMMENT   Although out of page sequence, these sections in total are an aside to the story and should be considered together. They deal with the incident where Daz becomes part of the indifferent violence of his society. The storyline has become action-packed and fast-moving as the time frame becomes compact. We see little difference between the vicious attitudes of both Dred and Domestic Security and sense the pervading atmosphere of fear they create. Note the use of black humour (see Literary Terms) to relieve the tragic situation.

GLOSSARY   **tucker stamps** government vouchers that can be exchanged for food
smasht drunk
kickout (also kickowt) people who have lost their citizenship and are expelled from the suburbs
lyke the clappers very fast

Identify the speaker.

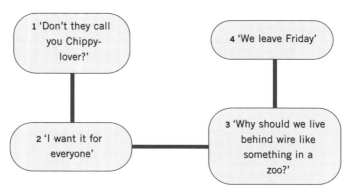

1 'Don't they call you Chippy-lover?'

4 'We leave Friday'

2 'I want it for everyone'

3 'Why should we live behind wire like something in a zoo?'

Identify the person(s) 'to whom' this comment refers.

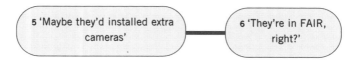

5 'Maybe they'd installed extra cameras'

6 'They're in FAIR, right?'

Check your answers on page 69.

 Consider these issues.

a The atmosphere of fear and violence created by the arrival of Domestic Security.

b How different Zoe's description of travelling through the tunnel is to that of Daz's.

c The reaction of people at Zoe's school to Tabby's expulsion.

d The government's right to segregate the communities.

e The effect created by the author's frequent references to cold in this section.

TOGETHER – LOVE TRIUMPHS AGAINST ALL ODDS (PAGES 112–165)

Pages
112–129

Zoe runs away on the Wednesday following the Wentworths' expulsion by stowing away under a trash truck. She is unsettled about leaving her parents but is determined to go.

What evidence is there that Zoe has behaved impulsively?

She feels she will be accepted if she brings luxury presents as gifts, but the determination and the sense of adventure soon dissipate when she arrives at the Rawhampton dump and is overwhelmed by panic. Having escaped Silverdale, her next task is to find the tallest building in Rawhampton and Daz.

Daz, meanwhile, has spent a cold and sleepless night. He fears Dred will come after him to avenge Pete's murder. He also feels guilty because he stole his mother's foodstamps. To make amends he trades Del's gun, the only item of worth he has, to buy food.

Think about the reasons why Zoe continues her search for Daz.

Zoe is out of place in Rawhampton: even neighbourhood children recognise her as a Subby from her patterns of speech and her revulsion (see Theme on The Effects of Environment) at kids playing with a dead body, and they set out to exploit her lack of experience. They cannot believe she left the Silverdale lifestyle voluntarily. As she runs they taunt her, and she

TOGETHER – LOVE TRIUMPHS AGAINST ALL ODDS

realises the danger they pose to her because of their lack of moral scruple and because she has been recognised as an outsider. Finding Daz is crucial.

The reality of the depth of poverty is a shock. Zoe accepts that Chippies are poor and that consequently their lifestyle is different, but she is totally unprepared for the degree of neglect she encounters. It's early November and the raw cold enhances the desolation. Meeting Daz and his mother does nothing to dispel the sense of alienation. Their apartment is shabby – peeling paint, broken windows, and no electricity, heating, running water or sanitation. Just by being there Zoe presents a danger. The following morning, Zoe discovers the family name is Barraclough and an unhappy Daz sets off to find Zoe a safe hiding place.

COMMENT   The author focuses on fine descriptive detail and contrasts the neat and tidy environment of Silverdale with the overgrown wasteland of Rawhampton. We have a graphic description of the poverty and its effect on people from the use of dark, depressed language. In a civilised society the discovery of the corpse should

Consider the purpose behind comparing the children to animals.

cause revulsion; here it is an exciting treasure trove. The children are described as rats since they scavenge what they can. Zoe has come from an ordered world of plenty where adults look after her. Here she enters a world where survival depends on putting self first – being ruthless, being tougher and stealing or taking what one needs. The children have learned these skills; Zoe realises she has not.

Why does Mrs Barraclough remain anonymous for so long?

Arrival at the apartment does nothing to dispel Zoe's fear as Daz and his mother fight over Zoe's presence. It is Zoe who is now in receipt of prejudicial comment and begrudged hospitality. In an effort to hold on to something familiar she toys with the sound of 'Darren Barraclough'. 'Daz' is a contemporary diminutive common in popular slang. 'Darren', on the other hand, sounds more dignified, more formal, more representative of the Subby world she has left behind.

GLOSSARY

Germolene brand of antiseptic cream
gismo a gadget, the function of which is not readily obvious
sussed identified

Pages 130–133

Zoe is appalled by the state of the apartment and how the Barracloughs live. Unsuccessfully she tries to hide her feelings. In the culture of Silverdale, a guest would be expected to bring the host a gift. She offers Mrs Barraclough the impractical gifts and is angered by the snub her patronising action receives. Mrs Barraclough explains the misunderstanding: luxury, an appeal to vanity, has no place in surviving the poverty of Rawhampton where a warm coat and stout shoes have more value than fancy soap and lipstick. Mrs Barraclough survives the poverty by taking antidepressant drugs.

COMMENT

Daz has lived in poverty all his life. In these pages we see him ashamed of something he is powerless to change. Zoe's impulsive actions are a sign of her immaturity and unhappiness. The interaction between Zoe and Mrs Barraclough is the first sign of warmth, human dignity and human need hidden just below the surface.

GLOSSARY

put me down belittled me
john euphemism (see Literary Terms) for toilet

Pages 134–143

Mr James, a Subby teacher and member of FAIR who works in Rawhampton, is the only person Daz trusts. Mr James agrees to hide Zoe in a loft at the school. Before delivering Zoe to the school they must escape detection from the police. Daz hides Zoe in the

basement. Believing her safe, Daz endures the police
searches for Zoe. One of the urchins, claiming the
reward, leads the police to the Barracloughs' flat. This
is a tense moment because Zoe has left her jumper
there. The apartment is searched with no result; the
Barracloughs are threatened, and the police leave.
There is a moment of light relief as Mrs Barraclough
reveals she is wearing the incriminating jumper – the
police missed it because it was so obvious. Daz then
faces more problems. He is threatened by Dred, as they
suspect he killed Pete and intend to avenge the death.
Both 'authorities' are after him.

COMMENT   The waiting is almost like a game of hide and seek.
There is an excitement about it but no fear. Once the
perfunctory search is over, Zoe feels overwhelmed by
the dirt rather than the danger. Note she cries for the
comforts she has left behind.

GLOSSARY   **spiel** glib speech

Pages
144–156

During the two days she is in hiding at the school there
is much police activity on both sides of the barrier. In
conversation with Mr James, Zoe discovers that school
is taught in shifts – education is a privilege not a right
in Rawhampton. On her second morning at the school,
Zoe is startled awake by a very angry Mr James – she
had sneaked down during the night to wash. Although
careful, she is still naïvely unaware of just how serious
the consequences will be for people caught helping her.

Link the fear Zoe
shows here to fear
in other parts of
the novel.

Mr James tries to make her see that whilst she will go
safely home, the others will face the death penalty. She
later learns that with the Wentworths expelled, FAIR
has lost its Silverdale leader, and Mr James reveals to
Zoe that Grandma was the founding member of FAIR
in Silverdale. In a letter to Zoe, Grandma sends a map
explaining where she is to go, a safe house thirty miles

from the city in Clanton Hills. On Saturday afternoon the police arrive at the school and Zoe bravely escapes by joining the surge of kids rushing from the building. She then makes her way back to the Barracloughs' apartment.

COMMENT   The story is approaching its conclusion and the pace (see Literary Terms) of events increases. We see the higher human qualities of tolerance, love and loyalty demonstrated, as strangers rally round to help. It is also a coming of age for Zoe. In the heated exchange with Mr James we see the enormity of what she has done and the acceptance of responsibility for her own actions. Zoe must escape Pohlman if other, innocent people are not to suffer. Again we share a moment of wry humour when Zoe eats the evidence in the best tradition of espionage.

GLOSSARY   **boogied** danced
zonked slept
'we are members one of another' biblical quotation from Ephesians Chapter 4 Verse 25
asphyxiating suffocating

Pages 157–165   Whilst Zoe is outwitting the police, Dred come for Daz. He hides in the basement and, though cornered, is

TOGETHER – LOVE TRIUMPHS AGAINST ALL ODDS

Link the different reasons Daz and Zoe have for crying here to other parts of the novel.

safe until Zoe is captured by Dred and used as ransom. Just as Cal is about to start torturing Daz, Lieutenant Pohlman arrives. In the ensuing gunfight, Zoe and Daz make their escape. Miraculously, both are unscathed and arrive on Pinkney Hill, overlooking the city as dawn breaks. Rawhampton and Silverdale merge in the half-light, and from the distance of Pinkney Hill and in the minds of Daz and Zoe, the differences that split their community are no longer visible.

COMMENT   The exaggerated pace (see Literary Terms) and tension are emphasised by the use of short sentences. The pace stresses the dramatic quality of the ending. Daz has to choose between saving his mother or saving Zoe. We feel the pathos (see Literary Terms) as Daz cries at the hopelessness of his situation. Cal enjoys the thought of torturing Daz. Cal is cold, inhuman, vicious and brutalised by the environment he lives in.

Ironically, rescue comes from an unlikely source, Domestic Security. In the shoot-out between Dred and the police, Daz and Zoe make their escape. The novel ends in hope rather than despair. Love, loyalty and courage triumph, suggesting that if the prejudice was conquered by higher human qualities then perhaps the city and its people might be reunited once more.

GLOSSARY   shroud cover, disguise as if for burial
skittering moving jerkily across the surface
fire-fight vicious gun battle where no quarter is given

Identify the speaker.

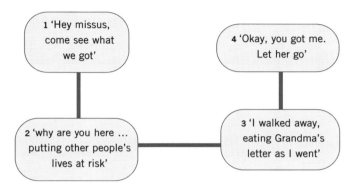

1 'Hey missus, come see what we got'

4 'Okay, you got me. Let her go'

2 'why are you here ... putting other people's lives at risk'

3 'I walked away, eating Grandma's letter as I went'

Identify the person 'to whom' this comment refers.

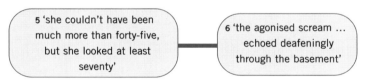

5 'she couldn't have been much more than forty-five, but she looked at least seventy'

6 'the agonised scream ... echoed deafeningly through the basement'

Check your answers on page 69.

 Consider these issues.

a The sequence of events that strengthens the relationship between Daz and Zoe.

b Acts of bravery, heroism and self-sacrifice.

c The role played by school in Rawhampton.

d The impact of revealing Grandma's connection with FAIR.

e The language used by the author to create a sense of hope in the closing pages.

PART THREE

COMMENTARY

THEMES

A theme is a unifying idea, image or motif, repeated or developed throughout a story. The following are four easily identifiable themes that can be found in *Daz 4 Zoe*.

LOVE

The title *Daz 4 Zoe* reflects the principle theme of love. The way in which it is written mirrors popular teenage graffiti, identifying the couple in a relationship. The way the young lovers first meet is reminiscent of the *Romeo and Juliet* story. Two young people, from feuding factions, see each other across a crowded dance floor. They fall in love at first sight, then risk ostracism and even death in order to be together.

Consider how the author portrays Daz and Zoe as sympathetic characters.

When they first introduce themselves, Daz is a very angry young man full of hatred; Zoe is very immature. As more events are revealed we see how their loving relationship changes them. They question the values of each respective society. Daz, no longer full of hatred, becomes a hero, brave, tender and gentle, yet still capable of an act of violence to protect someone he loves. Zoe becomes disillusioned with her world and rebels against it. As she begins to develop her own values, she regards the society she lives in as shallow, concerned only with material things. At first, for example, Zoe regards Paul Wentworth as important because of his wealth, not because he has done anything of value for others. She revises her opinion of him when she discovers he leads FAIR, fights against injustice and can provide sanctuary for Daz and herself.

Both Daz and Zoe love their families. In running away, Zoe knows how much she will hurt her parents. She asks Mr James to let them know she is safe, yet accepts that for the greater good, he cannot. Some kindness is shown when Grandma writes a secret message. Daz is very distressed at the thought of leaving his mother behind when Dred come looking for him. Daz and Zoe make difficult choices in order to stay together.

Notice how important strong, human qualities are to the development of the story.

The pressure by society and peers on people to conform puts enormous strain on the couple as they try to build a relationship in an almost impossible situation. They are from very different backgrounds, separated physically by barriers, culturally by parental disapproval and socially by deeply held prejudices and mistrust. Yet both are willing to make sacrifices to be together. Amid the poverty, injustice and violence, the finer attributes of humanity still survive – love, family, friendship and courage.

TOTALITARIANISM

Totalitarianism is an authoritarian system of government where only one political party is tolerated and which rules all other institutions completely. Such a system demands the complete subservience of the individual to the state and will not tolerate any opposition that threatens the lifestyle of the elite.

In the future world of this novel we learn that the 'Dennison government' introduced 'The Franchise (Income Qualification) Bill of 2004' (see pp. 41 and 42 of *Daz 4 Zoe*). As a result, the unemployed and low income wage earners lost the right to vote and therefore had no influence over government policy. The resultant destitute subculture became known as Chippyland. Zoe challenges the injustice of the system, but as Daz points out, 'they [the government] don't need the right 'cause they've got the power. They've got it forever too, 'cause only their friends get to vote' (p. 92). Subbies enjoy a comfortable, secure lifestyle. They automatically vote some representative of the party back into office to preserve that lifestyle.

Government maintains power by use of propaganda and violence.

The government's power is maintained by Domestic Security (DS) which maintains law and order. The authority of Domestic Security is absolute, its presence generating fear in Subbies and Chippies alike because of its private and public readiness to use violence.

The belief that DS knows 'everything about everybody' (p. 83) and the fear of swift, unquestioned reprisals against anyone seen as a threat to the state adds to their power. We see DS revoke the Wentworths' citizenship; we are told of the execution of Del; we experience the swift mobilisation of forces for the final fire-fight with Dred. There is no appeal to a higher authority because DS is that authority.

Not everyone is prepared to accept the totalitarian state. Peaceful resistance in an attempt to bring about change is typified by FAIR. Though ridiculed by many individuals and outlawed by the state, it presents a consistent effort to gain justice and a better standard of living for all. At the other extreme there is armed resistance by Dred – angry people attempting to force change. Action by either organisation requires great personal courage as personified by Grandma and Mr James on the one hand, and Del on the other.

The Dennison government may have been invented, but the governments of South Africa pre-1991 and of Chile (see Context & Setting) are examples of real totalitarianism.

THE EFFECTS OF ENVIRONMENT

'Flights and freeways link all suburbs, no matter how remote, but nothing spans the yawning chasm that lies between Veezaville and Chippyland' (p. 109).

Consider the descriptions of Silverdale and its houses.

The suburbs are securely fenced off and patrolled by armed guards to keep the two societies apart. Anyone legitimately moving between the two carries identification. Chippies need a valid permit and a uniform to enter a suburb in safety and they must leave before nightfall. In this way the Subby environment remains protected, the population prejudiced, arrogant and aloof. The Chippy environment, with its poorer levels of education and health care, and its high unemployment, is distant and easily ignored.

How realistic is the idea of environment affecting someone's behaviour?

The city environment portrayed by Robert Swindells is a frightening place, hostile and bleak. Through Zoe's eyes we see the difference between the orderly, clean streets of the suburbs and the squalor of the city. Zoe wonders how 'people could bear to live like this' (p. 16) and how Zena 'coped with the contrast between the beautiful house she worked in all day and the dump she went back to at night' (p. 79). These ideas suggest that Chippies have some choice in how they live. Only when Zoe experiences city life at first hand does she realise that Chippies have no control over their lifestyle. Mrs Barraclough survives her ghetto environment by taking antidepressant pills and accepting government charity; others steal or trade on the black market.

Consider the descriptions in the text of the Barracloughs' home.

Chippies feel abandoned by society. They don't bathe or use flush toilets because there is no running water; electricity and fuel supplies are interrupted so there is no heating; manual labour forms what little work is available and Chippies stay poor because wages are so low; streets and buildings stay unrepaired because there is no money for repairs; the children have no moral scruples. To survive they plunder corpses because a corpse has no further use for boots or clothes. With so much neglect and little chance of change it is perhaps not surprising that Zoe observes in their eyes 'That cold, dead look with something behind it like waiting' (p. 17) which reflects the anger, frustration and resentment Chippies feel. This same anger fuels an organisation like Dred.

For those determined to move between the environments, ways can be found. Travelling through the tunnel is unpleasant but forms a route by which Daz and Zoe can meet. The trash truck crew carry messages, for a price. FAIR infiltrate the city with Mr James. Attending school is a voluntary activity for Chippies, yet there is a waiting list for places because education offers a rare opportunity of escape to the suburbs.

PREJUDICE AND INTOLERANCE

The presence of economic prejudice and intolerance between Subbies and Chippies is central to the story. Although the story takes place in a Britain of the imaginary future, the historical background against which events are set is very important in making the story believable (see Context & Setting). Reference is made to the Falklands War of 1982 and popular music, so Miss Moncrieff's Modern History class discussing the Dennison government of 2004 is in context. It is also a turning point for Zoe, who rebels against 'brainwashing' and suffers taunts of 'Chippy-lover' as a result. Daz suffers a similar deadly insult of 'Subby-lover' because of his actions.

Consider the importance of the use of historical fact in this fictional novel.

It is to government advantage that the two societies are kept apart. Using prejudice to create fear is a cheap and effective method of preventing any change. Mr Askew's view that Chippies don't work because they get so many handouts is perhaps representative of the typical level of intolerance encouraged. Chippies in Silverdale are made easy to identify on sight. They wear blue baseball caps and blue coverall uniforms emblazoned with a large yellow circle. Without the correct 'seeit' they would be arrested immediately. Prejudice is responsible for the attitude that encourages ideas like: don't talk to a Chippy unless it's to tell them what to do, and don't walk on the same side of the street as a Chippy.

Think about other parts of the novel where prejudice is suggested. Media propaganda portrays all Chippies as evil, for example the newscast reporting four Fairlawn teenagers shot dead on a petrol station forecourt, and the handbills misrepresenting Zoe as kidnapped. Popular misconception is that Chippies will steal from a person then kill them because they are envious. Another popular misconception, this time held by Chippies, is that all Subbies laugh at Chippies and are snobbish, and all Subby girls who go Chippying are 'trash'. As her relationship with Daz deepens, Zoe begins to understand that Chippies and Subbies are alike, that there are good and bad people in both cultures.

STRUCTURE

The chapters in this novel have no sequential headings. The book is written with alternate chapters in the **voices** (see Literary Terms) of Daz and Zoe. Through conversational **flashback** (see Literary Terms), they explain, in **first-person narrative** (see Literary Terms), the same sequence of events from different perspectives. Through this technique of interacting the two conversational tones, we are drawn into the story. Zoe's contributions are longer and more detailed (for example on pp. 63–70 when she describes their meeting at the mouth of the tunnel). Often there are time-shifts within the sequence of events being recalled. When there is a break in the narrative or change in the tone of the information being imparted, Robert Swindells uses a symbol of two circles and a square (on pp. 5 and 17, for example) to highlight the fact.

Even when we know the environments are imaginary and the supposed events have already taken place, the structure used creates **willing suspension of disbelief** (see Literary Terms) – we are drawn into the story and accept that the events are unfolding as we read, for example during the final tense moments leading up to the gunfight in the basement. The **pace** (see Literary Terms) at which the plot moves on towards its happy conclusion, from the first meeting at the Blue Moon to the timely arrival of Pohlman to rescue Daz and Zoe from Dred, is largely due to the number of coincidences we are asked to accept.

DAZ

Handsome
Quick-witted
Physically strong
Resilient
In love with Zoe
Poor

Daz, full name Darren Barraclough, is one of the central characters in the book and shares the role of narrator. We see the world through his eyes as he describes events in **flashback** (see Literary Terms). He is a Chippy, one of the economically poor in the story. Loyal and caring, he lives with his mother in a dilapidated apartment in Rawhampton and they share moments of ironic humour in an effort to lighten their depressing lifestyle. He feels guilt at selfishly stealing foodstamps in order to get drunk. We also share moments of **pathos** (see Literary Terms) when he is upset by Zoe's reaction to the poverty he lives in and later when we see his tears as he hides from Dred. On both occasions he is powerless to alter the situation and we share his despair.

At fifteen years old he is resentful and angry at the way society treats its poor, and seeks membership of Dred – a violent terrorist organisation which kills Subbies – in order to take revenge. When he meets Zoe he falls instantly in love. We share his confused emotions as he comes to terms with his own prejudices and steps outside them, only to be ostracised by his peers. As their relationship deepens we see a gentler, more caring and mature person emerge. Zoe remembers his smile. She knows so little about him yet feels safe and protected in his company. Whilst Daz fears the viciousness of authority, he has a grudging respect for and trust in Mr James.

Resourceful, intelligent and brave, he uses what little education he has to plan a visit to Silverdale. His journey through the tunnel is dangerous and frightening but when he meets Zoe the effort is rewarded by the discovery that his love is returned. His resilience and determination are tested as he escapes the machine-gun fire of the security forces and again when Dred attack him for using the tunnel without permission.

We are reminded of the savagery and fight for survival that surround him when he kills Pete. Daz lives in a harsh world and this behaviour is acceptable under the moral code he has grown up with. The murder is premeditated and Daz is almost nonchalantly remorseless in response. Pete's death brings reprisals, and Daz is forced to choose between saving Zoe and protecting his mother. He acts with bravery and great personal integrity when surrendering to Cal in an attempt to secure Zoe's release.

Daz, in overcoming prejudice and mistrust, embodies some of the finer human qualities.

ZOE

Zoe, full name Zoe May Askew, is the other central character in the novel sharing the role of narrator with Daz. She is fourteen, and lives in the comfortable, secure world of the suburb of Silverdale with her parents. Zoe has few friends and bows to peer pressure to fit in. There is no doubt about her physical beauty and innocence; even in the crowded Blue Moon club, Daz is attracted to her straight away and knows she is different. The usual arrogant attitude of Subbies is absent.

Intelligent
Loyal to Daz
Sensitive
Attractive
Impulsive
Naïve

Zoe engages in **puns** (see Literary Terms) and generally demonstrates a more sophisticated style of narration. It is still conversational (as with Daz's narrative), and even with her use of Americanisms, it is closer to Standard English. She is more articulate than Daz, therefore her observations about other characters and the environment are often very revealing. For example, when she first visits the city we share her distress at the Chippy situation, and the anger in their eyes haunts her (see Language & Style).

Her role is important. She represents the need to question moral injustice and strive for a fairer society. Early in the story she repeats her father's prejudices *In what ways does* concerning Chippies, but soon we see her question *Zoe contrast with* society's preconceived ideas and challenge the prejudice *Tabby?* around her. As she thinks through the teachings of Miss Moncrieff's Modern History class she comes to the conclusion that she is being brainwashed. With provocative behaviour, that she tells us is out of character, she rebels against an unjust society to the point of getting into trouble at school, at home and with Domestic Security.

Most adults in the story treat Zoe as a child but we see, as Grandma does, Zoe growing towards adulthood as she learns to decide which issues are worth defending. Her belief in herself and trust in Daz come to be more important than the opinion of others. She learns that standing up for principles has a price and comes to see that people sometimes have to take great risks to defend things important to them.

Zoe sacrifices her comfortable lifestyle to be with Daz. Her relationship with Daz is one of mutual trust and support. They become equal partners in striving to escape the societies they live in and together promise a hope for the future.

Minor characters

Mr and Mrs Zoe's parents, Gerald and Amanda Askew, represent *Askew* middle class values. They are caring but cannot relate to Zoe's feelings. They are too accepting of the way society is. Amanda is a colourless housewife much

overshadowed by her husband. She is the family link to
Grandma and adopts the role of mediator. Gerald is
materialistic and believes his belongings, job and good
life in the suburbs are his by right. He lives very much
according to the values of his society. He despises all
Chippies and all things Chippy: he is a typical bigot
who reacts violently (see his outbursts on pp. 39 and 85
for example) to any suggestion that Chippies are in
any way equal to Subbies. On p. 5 we see an example
of how easily prejudice and intolerance can be passed
on from one generation to another (see Theme on
Prejudice and Intolerance). It is only Zoe's
independence of mind that saves her from perpetuating
the lies. Jealous of his reputation, Zoe's father cares very
much about public opinion. After a visit from Domestic
Security he overreacts and within a week has sold his
business and house to move to a new suburb.

Grandma   She is Zoe's great-grandmother. Despite her great age,
she is mentally alert and possesses great integrity and
strength of character. Living in a senior citizen's
apartment in Silverdale, she serves to illustrate the
difference in quality of lifestyle – for, had Grandma
been a Chippy, she would have died long before
reaching one hundred and four. Calm and self-
possessed, Zoe trusts her. Grandma understands the

value of silence when people are talking about an event that changed their lives forever; she listens without being judgemental. Unknown to the rest of the Askew family, Grandma founded FAIR in Silverdale because she knows the battle against prejudice and inequality cannot be won by brute force.

Tabitha Wentworth

Known as Tabby, Tabitha Wentworth is Zoe's best friend. She is rich, and her family are well respected in Silverdale because her father, Paul Wentworth, is not only a prosperous developer, but also chairman of a number of influential committees. By organising the 'Chippying' adventure, Tabby is the catalyst who makes it possible for Daz and Zoe to meet for the first time. Her behaviour and lifestyle are typical of the spoilt teenagers of Silverdale.

As the story develops, it becomes clear that Mr Wentworth secretly heads the Silverdale FAIR unit. The family are involved with so many committees because they are trying to gauge public opinion. When the FAIR connection is exposed, money and position cannot protect them from public rejection and they become 'kickouts'. At fourteen, Tabby seems to have everything in her favour: wealth, friends, excitement and security; but we see just how fragile and illusory these things are when she and her family lose their citizenship.

Mr James

Mr James holds a different set of values from Mr Askew and represents the changing attitudes of some Subbies. As a member of FAIR, Mr James is an enlightened man who recognises the wrongness of prejudice. He hopes that FAIR will triumph and that a more tolerant society will emerge. In the meantime he is trying to salve his conscience by teaching in the city. Unconcerned about his own safety, he does what he can to help Chippies and risks his life and position to help Daz and Zoe.

Miss Moncrieff

Portrayed as a sarcastic disciplinarian wrapped up in her subject, Miss Moncrieff is a point of contact for the teenage audience of the novel. A teacher we have all met and all love to hate: one with the smile of a shark and a stare that transfixes a class. It is her attitude that causes Zoe to realise the injustice around her and rebel.

Lieutenant Pohlman and Sergeant Daws

As representatives of Domestic Security they are feared figures of authority because they can revoke citizenship and throw people into prison; their job is to find and dispose of 'traitors', citizens who challenge the government. They operate on both sides of the barrier and seem to enjoy creating fear; power has rendered them amoral and they are unaware that they are doing anything wrong. They carry out their work with almost religious fervour. Pohlman interrogates Zoe, is present at the Chippy school and finally at the basement fire-fight. Zoe manages to outwit them each time, perhaps because they use brute force rather than reasoning.

Cal

Cal is considered a hero by Chippies; a legend in the fight against Subby oppression. But when Cal and Daz meet at the Blue Moon, Daz is amazed to find that his larger-than-life hero is only a 'littel guy wiv spex' who appears older than the other Dred members. Whatever warrior-like image Daz may have created of the Dred leader, he is disappointed by the reality of Cal's blond hair, age and neat appearance.

Small, nervous and unimposing, Cal is a typical bully: he rules by fear, yet runs at the first sign of personal danger. He is ruthless and savage, which can be seen in his evident enjoyment at the thought of torturing Daz. Operating outside the law, it is not hard to believe the merciless Cal is the vicious leader who masterminds Dred and has a reward of 50,000 dollars on his head.

Mick, Pete and Smithy	Minions of Cal, they enjoy the power that being members of Dred gives them. Pete's death shows us how cheaply life in Rawhampton is held.

Mrs Barraclough

Daz's mother pops pills to lessen the effects of 'dulleye', a **euphemism** (see Literary Terms) for depression. By hiding away in her apartment, she survives the almost intolerable living conditions and bleak city lifestyle of Rawhampton. Zoe compares her with a saggy, colourless armchair, thin, old and worn out – she is beaten into submission by fear, poverty and the hopelessness of her situation.

There is a **pathos** (see Literary Terms) about Mrs Barraclough's character which is shown in the matter-of-fact way she rejects Zoe's luxury gifts and in the humour she shares with her son. Her love for Daz is evident from the beginning of the story, but by the end of the novel even this cannot sustain her and she prefers to face Dred alone rather than attempt escape from the city.

Mr and Mrs Wentworth

Wealthy and supposedly powerful, Tabby's parents serve to illustrate how vulnerable all citizens who oppose an unjust and ruthless government are. Paul Wentworth took over as leader of the Silverdale unit of FAIR after Grandma considered herself too old for the job.

Ned and Larry

Ned and Larry are portrayed as 'models' of the typical Silverdale teenager. Although arrogant, opinionated and thoughtless, their behaviour is considered normal and well-balanced for young men of their time. The way they are represented allows us to contrast them with Daz, who in theory is their inferior but in reality is far more chivalrous.

Trash truck crew and Zena

As Chippies trusted to work in Silverdale, they cross the security fence into the suburb each day to perform menial tasks. They offer a contrast in lifestyles and

point up the inhumanity of a system that segregates its
citizens through prejudice.

LANGUAGE & STYLE

STYLE   Robert Swindells uses a narrative style of writing which
engages the teenage reader as his target audience. The
two main characters in *Daz 4 Zoe* are portrayed as
teenagers and the reader is asked to believe that they are
listening to Daz and Zoe as contemporaries, telling
their story in **flashback** as **first-person narrative** (see
Literary Terms). It is important that the language is
realistic and sounds like spoken English. In addition,
Zoe and Daz come from very different social and
economic backgrounds; as such, each character must
have a unique and recognisable **voice** (see Literary
Terms) to suit their circumstances. Descriptive detail is
used sparingly with great effect to emphasise the degree
of poverty in the city. Narrative style allows the action
to move at a fast **pace** (see Literary Terms), particularly
the moments of escape, and encourages **empathy** (see
Literary Terms) as the characters share their feelings
and emotions. This style enables Robert Swindells to
persuade the reader to question and challenge prejudice
that abuses human dignity and human rights.

USE OF LANGUAGE

Dialect   One of the first things we notice about Daz is the
simplistic way he speaks in present tense, **colloquial**
(see Literary Terms) English. Numbers are written as
figures rather than words and many words are spelt
phonetically; combined with use of **dialect** and
neologism (see Literary Terms), this is used to suggest
a poor level of education. In contrast, Zoe uses a more
sophisticated style of speech. Whilst the informality of

slang is still present, her contributions are longer, more grammatically correct and generally more descriptive.

Americanism and colloquialism

Language changes and grows almost like a living entity as words and ideas are absorbed from other cultures and traditions. In the futuristic world of *Daz 4 Zoe* we see the influence of contemporary American 'Popular Speak' which is popular with the youth of today. For example: Zoe uses words like 'guys', 'freeway', 'ma and pa', 'trash' and 'movie'. The speech patterns of the gate security guards and Mrs Barraclough are very Americanised too. In the **colloquial** (see Literary Terms) use of language we also see the reduction of words to their simplest forms – for example, 'Daz' and 'Tabby' are diminutives of 'Darren' and 'Tabitha' respectively.

Names

The names of the city and suburbs, organisations and clubs are used as **symbols** (see Literary Terms) to reflect pleasant and unpleasant characteristics. 'Silverdale', 'Fairlawn', 'Goldengrove' and 'Peacehaven' sound gentle and prosperous as opposed to 'Rawhampton' which sounds rough and poor. 'Dred' suggests an organisation to fear, whilst 'FAIR' suggests protection and a sense of justice. 'Blue Moon' and 'Black Diamond' cater for an adult clientèle and their names sound more enticing than 'youth club'.

Voice

The way in which Robert Swindells shows us a world of the future through the individual **voices** (see Literary Terms) of two teenagers is very clever. The technique of giving Daz a limited ability to describe the divided world yet at the same time allowing us to share his feelings is quite sophisticated. Zoe's voice fills in the gaps in description and story. The interaction of the pair gives the reader a more complete understanding of the plot. Our **empathy** (see Literary Terms) for Daz and Zoe and sympathy with their situation come about because of the manner in which the story is told.

PART FOUR

Study skills

How to use quotations

One of the secrets of success in writing essays is the way you use quotations. There are five basic principles:
- Put inverted commas at the beginning and end of the quotation
- Write the quotation exactly as it appears in the original
- Do not use a quotation that repeats what you have just written
- Use the quotation so that it fits into your sentence
- Keep the quotation as short as possible

Quotations should be used to develop the line of thought in your essays.

Your comment should not duplicate what is in your quotation. For example:

As Zoe walks down cracked and broken roads looking for Daz she describes the debris that litters the streets of Rawhampton. 'The streets were cracked and broken and littered with every sort of debris. Long puddles of foul, stagnant water lay in gutters clogged with filth.'

Far more effective is to write:

As Zoe searches for Daz in the unfamiliar city she describes the streets of Rawhampton as 'cracked and broken and littered with every sort of debris'.

The most sophisticated way of using the writer's words is to embed them into your sentence:

Zoe was unprepared for the 'gutters clogged with filth' as she walked the 'cracked and broken' streets in search of Daz.

When you use quotations in this way, you are demonstrating the ability to use text as evidence to support your ideas - not simply including words from the original to prove you have read it.

Everyone writes differently. Work through the suggestions given here and adapt the advice to suit your own style and interests. This will improve your essay-writing skills and allow your personal voice to emerge.

The following points indicate in ascending order the skills of essay writing:

- Picking out one or two facts about the story and adding the odd detail
- Writing about the text by retelling the story
- Retelling the story and adding a quotation here and there
- Organising an answer which explains what is happening in the text and giving quotations to support what you write

....

- Writing in such a way as to show that you have thought about the intentions of the writer of the text and that you understand the techniques used
- Writing at some length, giving your viewpoint on the text and commenting by picking out details to support your views
- Looking at the text as a work of art, demonstrating clear critical judgement and explaining to the reader of your essay how the enjoyment of the text is assisted by literary devices, linguistic effects and psychological insights; showing how the text relates to the time when it was written

The dotted line above represents the division between lower- and higher-level grades. Higher-level performance begins when you start to consider your response as a reader of the text. The highest level is reached when you offer an enthusiastic personal response and show how this piece of literature is a product of its time.

Coursework essay

Set aside an hour or so at the start of your work to plan what you have to do.

- List all the points you feel are needed to cover the task. Collect page references of information and quotations that will support what you have to say. A helpful tool is the highlighter pen: this saves painstaking copying and enables you to target precisely what you want to use.
- Focus on what you consider to be the main points of the essay. Try to sum up your argument in a single sentence, which could be the closing sentence of your essay. Depending on the essay title, it could be a statement about a character: Since Daz is prepared to risk his life to see Zoe again we cannot doubt the depth of his love for her; an opinion about a setting: The tunnel is a symbol of hope because it unites city and suburb; or a judgement on a theme: The effects that the different environments have on the people who live in them are plain to see. Yet, even the poverty and squalor of Rawhampton cannot crush the finer attributes of humanity like love, loyalty and courage.
- Make a short essay plan. Use the first paragraph to introduce the argument you wish to make. In the following paragraphs develop this argument with details, examples and other possible points of view. Sum up your argument in the last paragraph. Check you have answered the question.
- Write the essay, remembering all the time the central point you are making.
- On completion, go back over what you have written to eliminate careless errors and improve expression. Read it aloud to yourself, or, if you are feeling more confident, to a relative or friend.

If you can, try to type your essay using a word processor. This will allow you to correct and improve your writing without spoiling its appearance.

Examination essay

The essay written in an examination often carries more marks than the coursework essay even though it is written under considerable time pressure.

In the revision period build up notes on various aspects of the text you are using. Fortunately, in acquiring this set of York Notes on *Daz 4 Zoe*, you have made a prudent beginning! York Notes are set out to give you vital information and help you to construct your personal overview of the text.

Make notes with appropriate quotations about the key issues of the set text. Go into the examination knowing your text and having a clear set of opinions about it.

In most English Literature examinations you can take in copies of your set books. This is an enormous advantage although it may lull you into a false sense of security. Beware! There is simply not enough time in an examination to read the book from scratch.

In the examination

- Read the question paper carefully and remind yourself what you have to do.
- Look at the questions on your set texts to select the one that most interests you and mentally work out the points you wish to stress.
- Remind yourself of the time available and how you are going to use it.
- Briefly map out a short plan in note form that will keep your writing on track and illustrate the key argument you want to make.
- Then set about writing it.
- When you have finished, check through to eliminate errors.

To summarise, these are keys to success

- **Know the text**
- **Have a clear understanding of and opinions on the storyline, characters, setting, themes and writer's concerns**
- **Select the right material**
- **Plan and write a clear response, continually bearing the question in mind**

A typical essay question on *Daz 4 Zoe* is followed by a sample essay plan in note form. This does not present the only answer to the question, merely one answer. Do not be afraid to include your own ideas and leave out some of the ones in this sample! Remember that quotations are essential to prove and illustrate the points you make.

Daz and Zoe are attracted to one another. With reference to three moments in the story, show how their relationship develops.

Introduction

The story of *Daz 4 Zoe* follows the developing relationship, described in flashback by the author, between two teenagers who meet in unlikely circumstances and are mutually attracted to one another.

Reference 1 (pp. 20–30)

Meeting at Blue Moon. Daz attracted by Zoe's looks and attitude; she by his looks and heroism.
- Love at first sight; both determined to see each other again.
- Class differences and prejudices put to one side (describe different backgrounds of Daz and Zoe); love helps them see themselves as people rather than Subbies or Chippies.

Reference 2 (pp. 56–72)

Daz travels through secret tunnel. The journey is terrifying; Daz has no way of knowing what sort of reception he will get from Zoe.
- He is risking death (from security guards, etc.) but is driven by need to meet Zoe.
- By coincidence she arrives at tunnel mouth (explain why she is there).
- They discover their feelings are more than infatuation and arrange method of communication via the trash truck crew.
- A moment of chivalry leads to a moment of tension when guards open fire.

Reference 3   Daz and Zoe together in city; threatened by Dred.
(pp. 160–165)   • Daz offers to sacrifice himself for Zoe's freedom, a selfless act of heroism.
                   • Both saved by Lieutenant Pohlman, an unlikely rescuer.
                   • Story ends with their joint voice and the hope that city and suburb societies will learn to see the best in people, just as they have.

Conclusion   Daz and Zoe come from very different backgrounds and from societies that strongly disapprove of each other. Since they are together at the beginning of the story, we know from the start that the teenagers must have survived all the efforts of society to keep them apart. This resilience suggests the relationship they share is more than a teenage crush.

FURTHER QUESTIONS

Make a plan as shown above and attempt these questions.

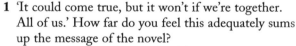

1 'It could come true, but it won't if we're together. All of us.' How far do you feel this adequately sums up the message of the novel?

2 Outline the contribution that THREE of the following make to the main plot of the novel: Tabby Wentworth; Grandma; Lieutenant Pohlman; Cal; Mr James; Zoe's parents.

3 *Daz 4 Zoe* is a love story. Consider how the author illustrates the following:
   • the happiness and unhappiness Daz and Zoe experience because of love
   • how differently people view things when they are in love
   • looking for the best in people
   • the language characters use to express their feelings of love

4 How does the author make us feel that this novel happens at some future date? In your answer you might wish to examine: use of language; setting; social structure; everyday background.

5 Compare and contrast the images of Rawhampton and Silverdale given to us by the author.

6 How far do you think that the presentation of teenagers is accurately reflected in the novel?

7 What do you think Robert Swindells tries to show us in the novel about each of the following:
   • the behaviour of Ned and Larry
   • the behaviour of Chippy children
   • the behaviour of Cal

8 Daz executes Pete, yet we still come to appreciate Daz as a sympathetic character. How does the author achieve this?

9 Find the passages where Daz describes travelling through the tunnel. Explain how Robert Swindells brings out the following:
   • how Daz feels at first
   • how his feelings change
   • tension and excitement
   • the importance of this journey in the novel as a whole

10 Why is Mrs Barraclough an important character in the novel?

11 Compare the ways in which TWO of the following treat Zoe: Grandma; Miss Moncrieff; Mr James; Mr and Mrs Askew. In your answer you should consider:
   • their attitudes and values
   • what they say and do
   • your reactions to them

12 What purpose do the illegal organisations Dred and FAIR serve in the novel?

13 Contrast the two systems of education described in the novel. Remember to include reference to the

pupils' reactions to school and events that interrupt a 'normal' day.

14 Domestic Security in *Daz 4 Zoe* is a government agency carrying out government policies. With close reference to the text explain their effectiveness in maintaining law and order.

15 How far does coincidence add to the pace of the novel? Outline, in some detail, TWO occasions where coincidence determines the action that takes place.

PART FIVE

CULTURAL CONNECTIONS

BROADER PERSPECTIVES

What if? Daz 4 Zoe is a novel which portrays a love story set against the injustice of segregation. The teenagers in this story rebel against what they see as false values in the society around them. Fourteen-year-old Zoe's refusal to unquestioningly accept government propaganda is even considered a threat to society. There are many stories that explore the possible societies and cultures of a future world. You may enjoy texts like *Fahrenheit 451* by Ray Bradbury; *Logan's Run* by William F. Nolan; and *The Machine Stops* by E.M. Forster.

Love stories One well known love story is the play *Romeo and Juliet* written by William Shakespeare. Texts are often changed slightly when they are adapted for different audiences and media. If the thought of reading a whole Shakespearean play is daunting, try a shortened, prose version of the text. You could try *Shakespeare Stories* by Leon Garfield (Gollancz, 1992) or Lamb's *Tales from Shakespeare*. If you prefer to hear and/or watch the play there are several screen versions of the *Romeo and Juliet* story available, the most recent being the 1996 film starring Leonardo DiCaprio and Claire Danes. A famous adaptation is Leonard Bernstein's *West Side Story* (1957).

Human rights Another issue you may wish to explore further is the idea of the injustice of segregation based on factors that people have little or no control over. *The Power of One* (Mandarin Books, 1989) is written by Bryce Courtenay and is an account of an English boy educated in Africa who, as he grows up, works to expose the injustices of apartheid. *The Power of One* is available as a video (1992) directed by John G. Avildson and starring Stephen Dorff, Morgan Freeman and Sir John Gielgud.

Two factual texts dealing with the subject of apartheid are *Causes and Consequences of the End of Apartheid* by Catherine Bradley (Evans Brothers, 1995) and *Children Under Apartheid* (International Defence and Aid Fund for Southern Africa and United Nations Centre Against Apartheid, 1980). Information on human rights can be obtained from Amnesty International, 99–119 Rosebery Avenue, London EC1R 4RE. The Internet address for Amnesty International's Web site is http://www.oneworld.org/amnesty/.

acronym a pronounceable word formed from the initial letters of other words (see 'FAIR' on p. 85)

black humour cynical amusement used to lighten unpleasant or potentially tragic situations

colloquial in common, conversational use

dialect a local version of a language, different in the way words are pronounced and used, for example 'dazzlers' (bright lights) and 'lornorders' (policemen)

empathy the sensation of mentally identifying with a person or character in a story, to the point of fully understanding their thoughts, feelings and actions

euphemism a mild or vague expression substituted for one thought to be too harsh, unpleasant or direct to use, e.g. Del was topped rather than executed

first-person narrative a story told from the point of view of an 'I' figure, a character directly involved in the action

flashback a sudden jump backwards in time to an earlier event, giving the reader a fuller picture because the past is described alongside the present

ironic pun humorous or mildly sarcastic use of words to imply the opposite of what they say, for example the play on the word 'Pal' on p. 16. Words spoken innocently but which later prove to be mistaken or to have prophesied an event are also classed as ironic

neologism invention of new words, where a meaning is suggested from the context of other words in the sentence. For example, 'Veeza-Teeza' on p. 14 refers to an exam

pace the speed at which the story progresses

pathos a quality in speech, writing or events that creates a feeling of pity or sadness

pun use of two very different meanings of a single word, usually for comic effect, as in 'Ded rong' on p. 61

symbol/symbolic an object or idea which, by association, represents something else. For example, the tunnel can be seen as a symbol of hope because it unites city and suburb

voice the person expressing an opinion or point of view. There may be more than one point of view offered in a piece of writing. Voice helps a reader to identify the different sources of opinion

willing suspension of disbelief the reader's acceptance of unlikely or improbable events or situations in a piece of writing as necessary for the development of the story. For instance, the number of coincidences allowing Daz and Zoe to meet, or escape danger, requires the willing suspension of disbelief on the part of the reader

TEST ANSWERS

TEST YOURSELF (Section 1 pp. 3–9)

A 1 Mrs Barraclough *(p. 3)*
2 Daz *(p. 3)*
3 Zoe *(p. 5)*
4 Daz *(p. 8)*
5 Mr Wentworth *(p. 4)*
6 Daz *(p. 7)*

TEST YOURSELF (Section 2 pp. 10–55)

A 1 Tabby *(p. 10)*
2 Mick *(p. 36)*
3 Miss Moncrieff *(p. 48)*
4 Zoe *(p. 53)*
5 Cal *(p. 23)*
6 Grandma *(p. 40)*

TEST YOURSELF (Section 3 pp. 56–76)

A 1 Daz *(p. 61)*
2 Zoe *(p. 64)*
3 Mick *(p. 76)*
4 Daz *(p. 76)*

5 Mrs Barraclough *(p. 56)*
6 Del *(p. 68)*

TEST YOURSELF (Section 4 pp. 77–111)

A 1 Lieutenant Pohlman *(p. 82)*
2 Zoe *(p. 84)*
3 Zoe *(p. 91)*
4 Gerald Askew *(p. 106)*
5 Domestic Security (DS) *(p. 90)*
6 Mr and Mrs Wentworth *(p. 97)*

TEST YOURSELF (Section 5 pp. 112–165)

A 1 a tiny, dirty-nosed girl [one of the gang who finds Pete's body] *(p. 120)*
2 Mr James *(p. 149)*
3 Zoe *(p. 156)*
4 Daz *(p. 161)*
5 Mrs Barraclough *(p. 125)*
6 Cal *(p. 162)*

Notes

NOTES

NOTES

NOTES

NOTES

GCSE and equivalent levels (£3.50 each)

Maya Angelou
I Know Why the Caged Bird Sings

Jane Austen
Pride and Prejudice

Harold Brighouse
Hobson's Choice

Charlotte Brontë
Jane Eyre

Emily Brontë
Wuthering Heights

Charles Dickens
David Copperfield

Charles Dickens
Great Expectations

Charles Dickens
Hard Times

George Eliot
Silas Marner

William Golding
Lord of the Flies

Willis Hall
The Long, the Short and the Tall

Thomas Hardy
Far from the Madding Crowd

Thomas Hardy
The Mayor of Casterbridge

Thomas Hardy
Tess of the d'Urbervilles

L.P. Hartley
The Go-Between

Seamus Heaney
Selected Poems

Susan Hill
I'm the King of the Castle

Barry Hines
A Kestrel for a Knave

Louise Lawrence
Children of the Dust

Harper Lee
To Kill a Mockingbird

Laurie Lee
Cider with Rosie

Arthur Miller
A View from the Bridge

Arthur Miller
The Crucible

Robert O'Brien
Z for Zachariah

George Orwell
Animal Farm

J.B. Priestley
An Inspector Calls

Willy Russell
Educating Rita

Willy Russell
Our Day Out

J.D. Salinger
The Catcher in the Rye

William Shakespeare
Henry V

William Shakespeare
Julius Caesar

William Shakespeare
Macbeth

William Shakespeare
A Midsummer Night's Dream

William Shakespeare
The Merchant of Venice

William Shakespeare
Romeo and Juliet

William Shakespeare
The Tempest

William Shakespeare
Twelfth Night

George Bernard Shaw
Pygmalion

R.C. Sherriff
Journey's End

Rukshana Smith
Salt on the snow

John Steinbeck
Of Mice and Men

R.L. Stevenson
Dr Jekyll and Mr Hyde

Robert Swindells
Daz 4 Zoe

Mildred D. Taylor
Roll of Thunder, Hear My Cry

Mark Twain
The Adventures of Huckleberry Finn

James Watson
Talking in Whispers

A Choice of Poets

Nineteenth Century Short Stories

Poetry of the First World War

Six Women Poets

Advanced level (£3.99 each)

Margaret Atwood
The Handmaid's Tale

William Blake
Songs of Innocence and of Experience

Emily Brontë
Wuthering Heights

Geoffrey Chaucer
The Wife of Bath's Prologue and Tale

Joseph Conrad
Heart of Darkness

Charles Dickens
Great Expectations

F. Scott Fitzgerald
The Great Gatsby

Thomas Hardy
Tess of the d'Urbervilles

James Joyce
Dubliners

Arthur Miller
Death of a Salesman

William Shakespeare
Antony and Cleopatra

William Shakespeare
Hamlet

William Shakespeare
King Lear

William Shakespeare
The Merchant of Venice

William Shakespeare
Romeo and Juliet

William Shakespeare
The Tempest

Mary Shelley
Frankenstein

Alice Walker
The Color Purple

Tennessee Williams
A Streetcar Named Desire

Jane Austen
Emma

Jane Austen
Pride and Prejudice

Charlotte Brontë
Jane Eyre

Seamus Heaney
Selected Poems

William Shakespeare
Much Ado About Nothing

William Shakespeare
Othello

John Webster
The Duchess of Malfi

Chinua Achebe
Things Fall Apart

Edward Albee
Who's Afraid of Virginia Woolf?

Jane Austen
Mansfield Park

Jane Austen
Northanger Abbey

Jane Austen
Persuasion

Jane Austen
Sense and Sensibility

Samuel Beckett
Waiting for Godot

Alan Bennett
Talking Heads

John Betjeman
Selected Poems

Robert Bolt
A Man for All Seasons

Robert Burns
Selected Poems

Lord Byron
Selected Poems

Geoffrey Chaucer
The Franklin's Tale

Geoffrey Chaucer
The Merchant's Tale

Geoffrey Chaucer
The Miller's Tale

Geoffrey Chaucer
The Nun's Priest's Tale

Geoffrey Chaucer
Prologue to the Canterbury Tales

Samuel Taylor Coleridge
Selected Poems

Daniel Defoe
Moll Flanders

Daniel Defoe
Robinson Crusoe

Shelagh Delaney
A Taste of Honey

Charles Dickens
Bleak House

Charles Dickens
Oliver Twist

Emily Dickinson
Selected Poems

John Donne
Selected Poems

Douglas Dunn
Selected Poems

George Eliot
Middlemarch

George Eliot
The Mill on the Floss

T.S. Eliot
The Waste Land

T.S. Eliot
Selected Poems

Henry Fielding
Joseph Andrews

E.M. Forster
Howards End

E.M. Forster
A Passage to India

John Fowles
The French Lieutenant's Woman

Brian Friel
Translations

Elizabeth Gaskell
North and South

Oliver Goldsmith
She Stoops to Conquer

Graham Greene
Brighton Rock

Thomas Hardy
Jude the Obscure

Thomas Hardy
Selected Poems

Nathaniel Hawthorne
The Scarlet Letter

Ernest Hemingway
The Old Man and the Sea

Homer
The Iliad

Homer
The Odyssey

Aldous Huxley
Brave New World

Ben Jonson
The Alchemist

Ben Jonson
Volpone

James Joyce
A Portrait of the Artist as a Young Man

John Keats
Selected Poems

Philip Larkin
Selected Poems

D.H. Lawrence
The Rainbow

D.H. Lawrence
Sons and Lovers

D.H. Lawrence
Women in Love

Christopher Marlowe
Doctor Faustus

John Milton
Paradise Lost Bks I & II

John Milton
Paradise Lost IV & IX

Sean O'Casey
Juno and the Paycock

George Orwell
Nineteen Eighty-four

John Osborne
Look Back in Anger

Wilfred Owen
Selected Poems

Harold Pinter
The Caretaker

Sylvia Plath
Selected Works

Alexander Pope
Selected Poems

Jean Rhys
Wide Sargasso Sea

William Shakespeare
As You Like It

William Shakespeare
Coriolanus

William Shakespeare
Henry IV Pt 1

William Shakespeare
Henry V

William Shakespeare
Julius Caesar

William Shakespeare
Measure for Measure

William Shakespeare
Much Ado About Nothing

William Shakespeare
A Midsummer Night's Dream

William Shakespeare
Richard II

William Shakespeare
Richard III

William Shakespeare
Sonnets

William Shakespeare
The Taming of the Shrew

William Shakespeare
The Winter's Tale

George Bernard Shaw
Arms and the Man

George Bernard Shaw
Saint Joan

Richard Brinsley Sheridan
The Rivals

Muriel Spark
The Prime of Miss Jean Brodie

John Steinbeck
The Grapes of Wrath

John Steinbeck
The Pearl

Tom Stoppard
Rosencrantz and Guildenstern are Dead

Jonathan Swift
Gulliver's Travels

John Millington Synge
The Playboy of the Western World

W.M. Thackeray
Vanity Fair

Virgil
The Aeneid

Derek Walcott
Selected Poems

Oscar Wilde
The Importance of Being Earnest

Tennessee Williams
Cat on a Hot Tin Roof

Tennessee Williams
The Glass Menagerie

Virginia Woolf
Mrs Dalloway

Virginia Woolf
To the Lighthouse

William Wordsworth
Selected Poems

W.B. Yeats
Selected Poems

York Notes – the Ultimate Literature Guides

York Notes are recognised as the best literature study guides.
If you have enjoyed using this book and have found it useful, you
can now order others directly from us – simply follow the ordering
instructions below.

HOW TO ORDER

Decide which title(s) you require and then order in one of the following ways:

Booksellers

All titles available from good bookstores.

By post

List the title(s) you require in the space provided overleaf,
select your method of payment, complete your name and
address details and return your completed order form and
payment to:

Addison Wesley Longman Ltd
PO BOX 88
Harlow
Essex CM19 5SR

By phone

Call our Customer Information Centre on 01279 623923 to
place your order, quoting mail number: HEYN1.

By fax

Complete the order form overleaf, ensuring you fill in your
name and address details and method of payment, and fax it
to us on 01279 414130.

By e-mail

E-mail your order to us on awlhe.orders@awl.co.uk listing
title(s) and quantity required and providing full name and
address details as requested overleaf. Please quote mail
number: HEYN1. Please do not send credit card details by
e-mail.

York Notes Order Form

Titles required:

Quantity	Title/ISBN	Price

Sub total _____

Please add £2.50 postage & packing _____

(P & P is free for orders over £50) _____

Total _____

Mail no: HEYN1

Your Name _____

Your Address _____

_____

Postcode _____ Telephone _____

Method of payment

☐ I enclose a cheque or a P/O for £_____ made payable to Addison Wesley Longman Ltd

☐ Please charge my Visa/Access/AMEX/Diners Club card
Number _____ Expiry Date _____
Signature _____ Date _____

(please ensure that the address given above is the same as for your credit card)

Prices and other details are correct at time of going to press but may change without notice. All orders are subject to status.

☐ *Please tick this box if you would like a complete listing of Longman Study Guides (suitable for GCSE and A-level students)*

York Press

Longman

Addison Wesley Longman